i

Blue Physics

Mary Lou Buschi

LILY POETRY REVIEW BOOKS

This book is dedicated to John A. Buschi.

Contents

Three

Blue

The way light bends—

      Blood through skin

A circle within

a lake—

      How it moves.

6/11/77

Dear Lucy:

You are probably confused, to say the least! I have been through Hell and back since you've seen me last. I couldn't begin to tell you what's happened! I truly believe we became very close friends in Nov - Jan and I hope the same still exists. If this is true please call me at 201-822-334 and I'll fill you in!

Love
John

3

One

The poem is always in your hometown, but you have a better chance
of finding it in another.

> —Triggering Town, Richard Hugo.

The low song a lost boy sings remembering his mother's call. / Not
a cruel song, no, no, not cruel at all. / This song is sweet. It is sweet.
The heart dies of this sweetness.

> — Song, Brigit Pegeen Kelly

The Ice Storm

Knocked out the power
leaving us camping
by the fireplace for weeks.

The velvet couches covered in thick plastic–
far off glaciers, Inuit families
living there, eating charred fish,
never fighting–never in anger. Our bedrooms,
mysterious caves left in wreckage.

The night before the storm, my brother
woke me, asked me for my coin
collection and anything
in my piggy bank, promised
he'd pay me back.

I got out of bed, felt the cold crack
like ice lightening up through my bare feet.
I was too young to understand
desperation. Too young to feel danger
while admiring the incomparable
beauty of a frozen tree in moonlight.

I imagined the Inuit family around a small fire
sharing stories, sharing how hard the world,
the mother stroking the chapped cheek of her
son who plays with a stick that he flicks
in and out of the flames.

My mother, a distant figure, walks the yard,
now a museum of glass, searches for her son.
Downed power lines edge the streets.
My father adds logs to the flames
that jump and lick to defy gravity.
The boy surrenders the stick to the fire.

My Mother Too Grief Stricken to Mother

My grandmother dug
into her deep wooden

dresser to find a worn
envelope filled with

my red curly hair.
She handed me the twisted

strands. *Silenzio non piangere.*
Guarda in alto, c'è un dio che ti ama

Silenzio non piangere. She wanted
me to know she saved some

discarded part of me.
She pointed toward the night sky.

The city so bright,
a blinking *Park Here*, the only light in sight.

Non sei solo. Non sei solo.
I was alone with my grandmother,

orbiting the kitchen, orbiting the bedroom
aiming at some cold invisible moon.

Coda

My family pretending to be normal—
I've always hated my birthday.

My father cooking chicken on the grill
until it was black, yet raw in the middle

after my brother, John disappeared
for the first time.

My grandmother smoking and sweating
on the back porch. My mother rocking

in her chair, staring at the black
and white TV barely visible

in the sun's glare. I was out
in the brown grass. It was a dry July.

I was hoping for a little bit
of joy, a Carvel cake

soft enough to cut, allowing its chocolate
crunchy bits to spill from the center.

II.
Dear Lucy,

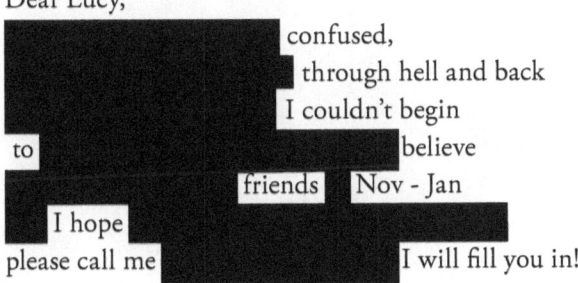

Love,
John

III.
There were no gifts, not even music.
Just the sound of the town parade,
trumpets, distant sirens, pounding drums
beating out some idea of American triumph.

IV.
Dear Lucy (~~Rose, My Love~~),

    Through hell, I've been.
This code—

      Please break it.
If we still exist.
      Love,
John

V.
I looked back at them, my father on the cracked
concrete step flipping terrible chicken,

peeling paint on the make-shift porch,
even the dog with her dry nose between her paws.

IV.
Dear

    I couldn't begin to explain.
I hope to see you   again
    on this side.
Love,

      John

VII.
A tableau of a family,
        how wrong
to think a family was like a body,
        a central heart,
it's really a tree, splitting
        from the weight of all that living.

Spring

Days before, we picked irises
from the rectory garden.

The buds leaned in and out
of the breeze—wanton little fists.

Our 4th grade teacher was not a nun.
She wore smart slacks, sweater sets,

kept her coal hair short, made us stand
at her desk, recite the difference between

there, they're, and their while steadying
a mid-heel Ferragamo on her big toe.

She never smiled. She ate graham crackers
out of a baggie, carefully tapping each

cracker before nuzzling it against her tongue.
It's opening! A quiet 4th grade watched a bud

yawn open. We knew, we'd never see something
this private, this small and strange,

as if a tiny elephant balancing itself on a thimble
was whispering into our teacher's ear, *miraculous.*

Falling

Lunch recess, a football tossed in the air.
Ben paced the length of the fence,

as a small group of girls gathered to gossip
about Duane and who he liked, while Ben

wanting so much to connect, ran at them
screaming "Ben germs" touching Cindy's back.

When the football soared too high, Ben jumped
up on a stone wall lost his footing, and impaled himself

on the wrought iron fence bordering the lot. The rod
one inch from his heart. Teachers rushed us back

into the building.
          In one version, the spike is a metaphor.

In another, we watch the medics pry Ben's

body from the spike, his leg twitching against the cyan sky.
          The truth, this happened to someone else, some asshole

who owned that schoolyard, survived, wore that scar
as a brilliant badge.
          So, the spike *is* a metaphor,

for how we broke Ben's heart everyday with multiple
tongues that carried the weight and viscosity of blood.

Kiss Kill

While sitting on the school's fire escape flipping sliced onions
off my sandwich, I thought about how I would answer
Kiss/Kill. Peg started it. We waited there every Tuesday
and Thursday for basketball practice to begin. Some
days the coach let us drive her car. We were in middle
school and the thought of being in control of anything,
especially a vehicle... I'd be in the backseat laughing
so hard I couldn't breathe as Peg tried to navigate the
church parking lot while coach screamed directives
at her. None us thought about gender, sexual
orientation, so when Peg told me to choose
someone I had to kiss and someone I had to kill,
I looked into the distance before taking another bite
of my sandwich. The Gingko trees had lost their
leaves and thankfully the stink-bombs they let loose
each spring were gone. Jim Depoe used the pods
as weapons to get the attention of the girl he loved.
I noticed the skin on my legs blooming with purple marks
as goose bumps gathered. *Answer the question.*
Peg's lips were full and slick. I imagined how soft they'd feel.
The rest of the team started to arrive, parents dropping them off.
I lived twenty yards from the church so I was on my own most days.
Kathy was a few steps away, waving when I felt Peg
staring me down. *It's late,* I said. On her way down
the fire escape, Peg punched me hard in the back.
To kiss is a touch. To kill is the death of that touch.

Girls

In Catholic uniforms,
hornets in their mouths,
they go down to the basement,
where Mr. Rosa, the school custodian,
is finishing up for the night.
His hands sliding around the long wet strands
of yarn to wring out his work.

Mr. Rosa lived with his daughter
in the rectory.   He spoke little
English.

Did he understand the girls' game?   Blouses unbuttoned
to the edge of their bras. Taunting him—playing victim.

Most nights they'd sneak back into the school
to climb through the vents, crawl under the stage,

an infestation of girls. Mr. Rosa would yell at them to get out until
he learned to play along,

jump out from dark corners—laughing and yelling in a language
the girls ridiculed. The truth, he could have been my grandfather,
uncle, or even
my father   but he wasn't.

After the basement descent, I watched him from the classroom window.
He walked down the hill to some other job.
Their brag rapped inside my ears.

A blue car driving slowly past—
the width of sky torn
from his daughter's ruled tablet.

To Snake a Drain

Brenda sobbed when she found her Kork Ease sandal
          jammed into the toilet.

It all happened between English and Gym
          in the second floor bathroom.

No one came forward to say that they had done it.
Was someone playing catch over the bathroom stalls?

Did Brenda do it herself?

You may have to apply pressure as you rotate the auger
around the tight curve into the trap.

Brenda denied the claim.
          The new custodian fished the shoe
out and put it in a plastic bag.
          Brenda was wrecked and what a shame,
her hair was in such a perfect twist
          on top of her head.
Her sweet face looked even more honeyed
          wet with tears.

If you don't feel the auger breaking
through and twisting getting easier,
pull the auger out.

Brenda receiving first-rate attention from teachers
          and students alike, sat up front the rest of the day.
I sat back braiding my thoughts around who
          could have done such a thing to so sweet a girl.

Search

We filed off the bus, greeted
        by once snarky teens wearing love beads
and sun kissed faces. My friend, so giddy,
        even her freckles sparkled,
handed me sheets and towels,
        showed me to my room
fit for a monk.

I was meant to stay there until lunch,
        with one small window
and my ludicrous humanity.

We ate white bread and American cheese,
        got into a circle, danced to *Get Together*
by the Youngbloods.
        The search leader, Sarah, our track star
at the high school never looked at me,
        which was perfect,
I was invisible, so when she hugged me,
        I wanted to rip my skin off.

That night I forgot the sound of my own voice
        after so many hours alone.
What I could hear were kids sneaking
        out, Sarah, gently knocking
on the chosen ones' doors.
        I watched them slink off to skinny dip,
smoke pot, have sex in the field.

I never wanted to come on this search, with its
        benevolence, self-actualization, and love.
Not everyone wants to be found.
        I was meant to let the grass grow
over me, a landscape to bury other bodies.

In right field missing that pop up,
        fixing my eyes, after I slipped,
to watch the clouds hover—
        even as the team screamed, "Get Up!"

Tangerine

We run past the smashed and jagged gravestones. Pebbled tar sticking to our bare feet. We call it conditioning; making the soles of our feet so tough we can walk on any surface without shoes. Laying out on the hood of my father's car, memorizing the lyrics to Tangerine. *Measuring a summer day:* skateboards, bikes, train rides between towns. No one knew where we were or what we were doing. It's the quiet car. He slips his hand up my shirt. I play dead. The game is whistle. Go as far as you can before *she* whistles. 1976, the bicentennial. Gerald Ford, is president. Underage drinking in cars is tolerated. Seatbelts, just ropes in metal cages. Jimmy Page is God. Children know how to entertain themselves in the basement during an adult party. Outside the basement window, we watch branches twist together, scratch an incantation. A Cardinal with one wing whispers our names.

Abecedarian

After Insley hats were banned,
        I began opening the second
button on my white Peter Pan blouse
        as a form of rebellion.
Could have been the folk masses,
        the relentless brown plaid,
detention for every day late,
        that made me start the group against
enlightenment. Who needs forgiveness anyway?
        Sister Evangeline
Francis made sure to remind me that,
        even with
guidance from "above" I chose to listen
        to a team of sinners waking in a
half darkened wood
        where I felt unafraid.
It wasn't until the priest,
        the one who smelled of
Jovan Musk, giant gold pinky ring
        with a Tanzanite stone capturing a
kaleidoscope of light,
        corralled only the girls after
lunch to garner
        our interest in a
monastic life that I banned Catholicism
        from my consciousness. This priest,
noting our skepticism,
        droned on about how
"Only the Good Die Young"
        was a song making fun of our
purity, yet he spent Sundays after mass
        visiting lonely housewives on
Quaaludes. I was not so much disillusioned
        because that would imply that I didn't

realize it was all a scam. The free rent.

    The free food. The free clothes all while
soliciting our commitment,

    just to lock us away in a nunnery. But that wasn't it.
The real hypocrisy was confession.

    If God's
ubiquitous, why confess anything at all?

    How is confession only
valid if spoken to this middle man?

    I lied most days because I had nothing to confess.

While the Cathys kneeled,

    I was having real discussions with God. E-
xample: God, honestly, what could he be thinking?

    Girls like us?
You can be honest. No one is listening but me.

    We both know the wine is sweet and I have
zero interest in bullshit and the chalice is empty.

The Head

Our high school biology lesson once
belonged most likely to a Chinese soldier.

It was dry, wrapped in parchment,
kept in a closet between two classrooms.

It had been ban-sawed in half
so we could open it like a hinged box or locket.

I held the cheeks turned wooden
in my palms, fingered the torn skin

where a red piece of rope remained.
Examined the lids scarred shut.

As the head was passed from hand-to-hand
Mrs. Stoutman intoned, "Too bad, so sad,

Mr. Peking man—Too bad, so sad."
Symptoms of asphyxiation: a loss of power,

heart rate slows, licks of light ringing in the ears.
What if it had been a gunshot wound,

like my brother's, the lead gliding past the hair
and skin opening upbraided and back rimmed,

but it wasn't. We learned nothing about anatomy,
but I held it, turned the head over and examined it.

Proof that he was real, once a man—now his countenance
an abyss for each one of us to climb inside. And we did.

Spotting

In the passenger seat of Colleen McGowan's car, she is doing donuts on the grass in the make-shift park, overgrown with Bayberry—Janet Jackson's *Pleasure Principle* on volume 10. I had always thought Colleen was one of the quiet ones, not like the girls who ran through the hallways. Yet, there we were spinning, fueled on volume and speed. But I was used to this…My home was a Rotor, that centrifugal death ride. I fixed my gaze on the lower right-hand crack in my bedroom window while the details of my brother's death flashed. I knew if I shut my eyes I would fall, but today I let go. Leaned into the spin. The vertiginous world a swath of colors. Maybe we'd hit a tree, wreck our faces on the windshield, run our fingertips over the embedded glass. *It's better you know what I thought was happiness was only part-time bliss.* And just like that, Colleen pulled the car out of the spin and drove into the straight away.

Last Will and Testament

Bette promised her ticket to Africa to Meera;
       Ian, a body and a real face to Mike.

Paul left his apologies for breaking
       a window in C hall to Mr. B.

Deanna, yellow jelly-beans to Gretchen,
       and a memory cube to Katz.

My father left a box of broken watches,
       42 hammers, and a bin labeled, *junk.*

My mother, 10 lipsticks, 3 feather dusters,
       6 magazine subscriptions and a drawer full of
Prozac and Ambien.

John left a resignation letter to
       the Bayley Ellard administration firing back
at the lack of support for both teachers and students
       and a letter to his students–

December 13, 1971

      Remember to follow the person
         who is searching
     for truth, not the person
         who claims to have found it.

A few photos from his short time
       in Jamaica, after we saw him for the last time,
a car key, and an empty briefcase.

When I unpack my breath,
       to my love I will leave the blue
              soft stitched linen my grandmother wove,
Sogni Doro,
       and a patch of flesh from an angel's hip.

Two

I looked down the length of the Vine. It was a long, narrow place, like a train car that wasn't going anywhere.

—Denis Johson, *Jesus' Son*

Body Parts Messenger
—For V. B.

You take time off from school,
        find an employer
that pays you to make deliveries
        using your own car.

You thought it was just a detour.
        You veered past a man
using a jackhammer, still hypnotized
        by the endless catalog of houses
and strip-malls, until finally,
        an open highway. German Techno
jettisons out of your open window,

        You accelerate into late September,
before you forget, your real name, this place
        giving in to what you have been ferrying,
as you turn the ignition off,
        to deliver one last pulsating heart.

Freaks Like Us

After playing in a photo booth, off season
on Coney Island, we followed a red narrow

hallway to a stage. A little person cracked jokes, a man
hanging weights from his stretched skin,

and a woman with burns all over her thighs
twirling fire batons. My drunk friend, Fraggle,

who could never deal with silence, talked nonstop.
Some people wore 3D glasses,

We didn't have those. I left feeling dirty.
I had forgotten entering the pier with my parents

at the end of the Atlantic City boardwalk, now
it returns like a riptide. There she sat, a bearded

woman, her eyes cracked walnuts.
I wanted to ask her if she ever heard of the Elephant Man,

who had to place his monstrous skull on his knees or risk dying
of asphyxia, but no one else was talking. We watched a movie

about him at school, him screaming, "I am not an animal!"
I wanted to tell her that we aren't so different, and, in fact,

we are all animals. I wanted to share that I had a dilation and curettage
when I was nine, a D&C, which is why I asked to have my breasts removed.

How many fields did I lie back in, shut my eyes and wait until
I swallowed the dark and endless winter? I wanted to tell this woman

sitting in front of me, offering herself as spectacle, that when
The Elephant Man decided to lie flat, he did so because of a poem

his mother read to him: Tennyson's, "Nothing Will Die."
My love, you are too good for this world.

Memento Mori I.

Nuns are sadistic, especially the ones who don't wear habits. Our principal's face was wool; her hair the texture of rusty Brillo. I sat in her office while she phoned my father. Her goldfish making quick circles, to the left, to the left, to the left.

*

It's November. My middle brother has died. We decide on cremation. Burning a dead body until no hands and feet are left, just ash. I put my hand inside the bag —

He's thick luscious sand. I want to walk on him, toss him in the air, make sand art in a jar by dying sections of him Cadmium yellow, Prussian blue, Vermilion, and Rose, take a long straw, make waves out of all his brilliant colors.

We didn't cremate John. No, my mother needed to see him whole one last time.

Today we stand at an open grave. The priest says what priests say, blesses the urn with holy water.
Rust rivers run down its sides, decomposing
before we have a chance to bury it.

Memento Mori II.

My mother holds up a blue beaded dress, *bury me in this*. I was eight. I used to climb into her closet to roll my fingers over the beads— remember, this dress, the sequined stars.

When she died, I chose a serious black suit with a white peplum. A dress for a magic trick: woman about to be sawed in half through the roof of her box. Before the funeral director closed the lid, he asked if I wanted the shoes back. I took them leaving my mother barefoot.

For months, I was trapped in a hearse with her. Window–Window– Door. I knew they were there, but I was inside the box, the open mouth of her shoes hooked in my right hand; a blue dress pinned like a dead bird above.

Gettysburg

It's as if Colin Meloy let loose the birds
from the branch and commanded the clouds
to descend at a speed that speaks to my inner
desire for flight.

*

We arrive on Culp's Hill, which played a prominent role
in the battle of Gettysburg; two rounded peaks,
separated by a narrow saddle. We stand there imagining
the dead and half dead being eaten by wild pigs.
I adjust the lens aperture, see a puffy white kid
in a Union hat, then purple buds clinging tightly
to a branch they look like frenzied insects—
My husband shouts, *"Did you get that?"* Yes. Yes, I did,
the branch, the buds, and the boy. *Where has he gone?*

*

The rifle revolutionized the war,
bullets circling the inside of the barrel
improving their accuracy.

*

Devil's Den, a field with craggy stones
where people convince themselves
they see something; feel a cold spot, a heady scent.
I shoot headlong into the expanse of it.
There is no focal point, shapeless, nameless,
and when we edit these photos later this will be the one.
Maybe it was just sand kicked up by a circling tire,
or a slow shutter hesitant to click shut?

*

Facts: There are more than 1,400 monuments,
markers and tablets at Gettysburg. More than 30,000 dead

and wounded soldiers were left in the wake.
More than one-third of all known photographs
of dead soldiers on Civil War battlefields were recorded here.

*

Tell me again why we've come?

      Come the war.

Come the rifle.

              Come the attrition.

Come the night.

      Come the voices.

Come the dead.

         No birds or boys in sight.

The Union of Heaven and Earth

An afterschool program for the uniquely abled. Rahi makes a card.
Shortest month. Month of gray snow and forcing bulbs. He uses very
little water, swirls his brush in the scarlet paint. His blazoned heart
shocks and pulsates. He adds pink lips, a sticker from a Family Dollar.
"Who is this for?" I ask. He continues to work. "Nobody," he says. His
right knee moves back and forth. He whispers addresses, train lines,
connecting buses across town. "Rahi, who would you like to send your
heart to?" I ask. "Nobody," he repeats, and I remember what Odys-
seus said as he stabbed the Cyclops in the eye, "I'm Nobody!" And the
Cyclops screamed, "Nobody has wounded me!" No one came to his
rescue, as his one eye sizzled around a stake until it burst.

Dear Somebody,

Nobody is asking
for open arms, a heart,
or to be mine.

I Saw a Girl

At a red light.
     A man
             swatted the phone
from her hand,
      growled something
I couldn't hear,
       shouldered her back
onto the sidewalk,
       while another man held
open the gate to a building.

I couldn't tell.   I couldn't tell
       what their relationship was.
As she walked,
      head down,
I noticed
      her broken sandals.

I couldn't tell her
      I know how impenetrable
male power is and
      how I wished
to give her my shoes
      made for running.

The light
       changed,
convection waves
      blurred the row houses
across the street.

Train Ride Through Small Towns

After Edward Hopper *Compartment C Car,* 1938

My suitcase,
        too wide for the aisle,
too heavy to lift.

I stood between
        the train locks,
where the breeze
        angles up,
where weeds between
        the rails cleave
to a purchase.

Wicker seats give
        and crack
as passengers sit.

The windows open,
        green fans wobble overhead.
A crowd gathers behind me.
        Heads turn to watch.

The train lurches forward
        into the summer fog.
There is more than
        enough unhappiness.

Grey History

The first morning I let Max out
on a long lead, we hear the cries,

the *gekkering.* Strangers among
the tangled vines, layers of sodded

leaves, pachysandra choking the hill.
The hair on Max's back, a raised narrow path—

beast knows beast. How to trace our steps back
into the purple darkness. Oh Coy-Wolf, Fox,

beautiful brute we mean you no harm
as you live wild between the Knotweed,

giving birth to pups who will only live 3 years.
You will have mange, eat field mice,

stay in your pack, called a leash.
You may be dead as I'm writing this?

In one version of this morning,
I meet your cries with my cries,

in another we are both quiet,
leaving space for the other.

Terrified for this World

Two young boys on Motocross bikes fly past me. One jacks his front tire and spins to a stop. They crest the hill and mud ridge reminding me of my adolescence. Anywhere was mine. I never let the "body of Christ" melt on my tongue. I chewed through the bland nothingness and proudly swallowed. Amen.

Still a few feet from me, one boy says, "Look how beautiful" The other looks in his friend's direction and says, "Yeah." They reach into their jeans. Grab cell phones, snap photos. I see a clear shot out to a dark and roiling river.

Baby Shower

We went in knowing we were hated through a cellophane prism of light. Bags with bears, a fox, an elephant in a box, a clothesline hung with tiny clothespins. Mothers floating in and out, the uterine fluid buoying us all. When the current turns to riptide, speaking different languages of love, a mother's mother offers me a slice of baby cake. I ate. I ate and ate—ignoring the soft belly, the light pink icing, whipped cream frothing from its center. I ate. I ate and watched the expectant mother giggle at the toes and chubby curves of the ankle and calf as she brightly nuzzled the sweetness past her lips. I am not a mother. Never will be a mother. Watching her tuck what was left of the crumbs and icing, the right arm, part of the shoulder under a blanket of sugar, careful not to touch the face, suspending her disbelief. The baby-still whole and sleeping there.

In Case of Emergency

In case of emergency / pull / the handle back / as the air grows thin / the pilot / *That's all -- That's all* / Will you choose the children first / help the mothers with their life vests / put your oxygen mask on / keep cool as the panic of others grabs / you / knowing that the black box / with its inscrutable brain / will tell the whole story / You will have several minutes / before hypoxia dims your memories / It was you who rubbed / Silly Putty / deep into the tweed sofa / lied about it / resulting in your brother's / broken engagement / You who French kissed Pat / before he was ready to open his mouth / And you who broke / into St Vincent's / stealing the bag of hosts / to give out at recess / *This is the body of Christ.* / *Amen* / And you / who thought while boarding this plane / you've had enough. / ~~Do it~~ / Open the metal rib cage / toss the others out / like paper petals / before the sudden / decompression / tears the roof off / watch each one of them sink into the unrest of the ocean / Gulping / every / one / down. / Yes, you say / I promise to know where / ~~to end~~

-

I Turned Thirty

In the basement of a ruddy
        Moroccan bar.

My father had just died
        after I asked him not to.

It was one of those premonitions
        on the way back to the airport,

both of us crying for no reason,
        getting lost in traffic on a boiling

day in Florida. He says, "ok."

Three

It is with deep regret that I must leave you, but rest assured it is in person only.

> —John A. Buschi, Resignation Letter to
> High School Students.

Can You See The Real Me
> —The Who

The Cyclone

When my father asked me
to ride the roller coaster at Bertrand's Island,

when I was too small, I acquiesced.
My mother disappeared into

the Tarot reader's purple tent. We knew
we had at least 15 minutes to sneak away

and ride the one mile of track with its sudden
dips and turns propelled only by gravity.

My father slipped me by the large vertical
ruler to quickly board a metal car, which back then

had no door, just a flimsy belt that stretched over our laps.
I curled myself into my father's chest, shut my eyes.

Both of us, silent. My father held on to the metal bar
with one hand and me with the other.

When the car lurched forward, some screams,
some laughter broke through the whip and crack

as the car careened over the track. After resisting
the force against my small frame, the final descent.

It felt as if we had put ourselves on a platform
at the top of the world and jumped.

There my mother was at the exit ramp.
I don't know if my father had any fun at all.

1991

Jailed █████████████████ *Two More Killings*

Convicted ████████████████████ *Spataro today was indicted by an Erie County grand jury in a 1981 Hamburg contract killing* ██

Spataro, 58, formerly of the Town of Tonawanda and Buffalo, is already imprisoned for two murders.
██ *charged with second-degree murder in the Feb. 1, 1981, shooting of Buffalo restaurant manager Robert Warner in a Hamburg parking lot.*

Warner, 32, also known as Robert Buschi, was shot once in the head

over a romantic grudge.

prosecutors said.

Dear Lucy,

I chose a name you would recognize - my father's name.
    I couldn't begin to explain.

How I've missed my life.

Love,

   John

The Day Room

In the middle of my life, I find myself back in high school,
where, years ago, I swallowed a handful of pills, landing
in a psych ward for two weeks. A small upright

piano in the day room waited to be remembered.
I knew how to play: *The Way We Were* and
With a Little Help from My Friends.

With patients my age I watched daytime TV,
ate vanilla ice cream out of white cardboard cups
with flat wooden spoons-deemed safe enough for us.

James admitted that he tried to hang himself multiple times.
Hanna said nothing. She held her Telecaster on her lap
like body armor, just strumming. Through windows

I watched the cars pull in and out, a Mondrian painting,
making and unmaking itself. I thrashed in anger, spoke in
tongues, as the doctor took notes.

Without warning, my parents stood in the door frame,
frightened of me, a new animal. As we walked down the hall,
Hanna joined us, played Joe Cocker's version of

With a Little Help From My Friends on her guitar. James turned
his face away from me. I was leaving him in the day room.
Maybe it was that my parents lied, told me my brother

was hit by a car, rather than shot in front of his car.
Later, I'd read my brother spent one week in a coma,
no one knew his real name, his alias, Robert Warner.

My father switched on the radio in the car. My mother hummed,
her voice, pin pricking the air. All these years later,
teaching Newton's Laws, it's James I think about most. He wanted to fly

but kept falling back to earth. I hope he is somewhere scattered,
a billion atoms, the thickness of a sheet of paper, that when released
floats ever so gently, resisting the pull of this world.

Black Maria

For years I dreamed you were alone
        in a cheap hotel room.
I'd drive there to find you
        but when I opened the door you were gone.

John, who would you be now? You at 75
        and me waiting 42 years
the cards yellowed in my hands.

Let me deal you in – The game of Hearts.

You with a full head of hair, crooked smile.
        Remember, Ace's are two points.

No player can play a Heart card
        or the Queen of Spades on the first trick,
A player can't lead with a heart
        until a heart has been "broken,"
or played in the game.

Should we order in, your favorite, dumplings?

John do you feel the sun?
        It comes in everyday at this time.
Lights up the splintered table.

Both of our faces bright—
        No distance between us.

When a Student So Sure I Know Nothing Screams, *You Need Jesus!*

I knew a man who was sure he had Jesus until his baby died in the crib. His wife could not stop cupping the baby's heart to find what they had missed. He looked at me while sliding on his shoes and said, *Is it that we didn't pray hard enough?* I imagined the anglicized portrait of Jesus, fine nose, shining mane of chestnut hair, clear white skin and that enlarged anatomical heart in his hand ringed with a crown of thorns, flames rising to the horizon of a cross. We stayed there for a while watching the light falling snow grow over fallen pine cones making sudden sepultures.

The Day We Heard They'd Take My Father's Leg

Worse than hearing he died. How will he drive the Wagoneer without a foot for speed? How will he climb the stairs to my bedroom to say good night, or walk me to the 5:26 train in the morning? The dead leg hung like an abandoned cliff. We carried on over it, making believe that it was not a tenuous line that had been crossed.

My father pulled rabbits from his toolbox; gray, white, brindle, all where there should have been hammers and screwdrivers. He offered me a Long Eared Lop Rabbit to screw in a socket. When he placed the rabbit in my hands it turned to sand. He said, "You see, it all happens that fast."

The morning of the amputation my father climbed out of his body, got behind the wheel of his big white van, waved back at us with a placid smile, disappearing into a flask of light.

The Day We Didn't

I ordered the drugs from Canada.
Unpacked the video.

Placed the syringe needle tip toward the TV.
I made the sheep dung tea as instructed.

Opened all the windows and doors to
let the peaty brew exhale from

one window to the next.
Unwrapped the packets of mixed vials.

Sat next to my mother to watch the video,
while encouraging her to drink

the muddy liquid. We watched in silence
facing the set. A woman calmly opens

her legs to allow her partner to inject
the serum into a main artery.

Shoulder to shoulder we lean in.
The video ended. Her tea gone.

I packed the vials, capped the syringes,
wrapped the video and sealed the box,

looked into her eyes, sat back down,
untethering each of us from hope.

Cactus

It was a relief to leave
        the weight of her to the day nurse
whose broad hands could lift,
        clean, and dress.

Soon, I will call you to sit in silence,
        both of us losing a role as daughter.
Tomorrow I will make a chair of my body
        stiff, expectant for her restless flesh,
which had become an empty cage.

We are daughters holding
        an umbilical cord left like a fossil of escape,
saved for years in layers of freezer ice,
        growing thicker each time the air hits it.

Turning

There is room enough for two
in your bed, but I stay off to the side

wanting to pull just one corner
of one blanket over myself.

Instead, I reach my arms around you,
pull the blankets in tight,

curl you up as if I was meant to send
you somewhere dangerous.

When by habit, or maybe will,
you try to cover my arms

as if the child you remember
is still here.

I Want

After William Blake

Ground brown sugar; black grackle feathers by the hundreds; the short wooden body of a ukulele; a perfect oil stick that can roll over paper like blue sky; saffron by the armful; the distance of every horizon from the tip of every sail; the deep hard laugh of my best friend; Scotch Bonnet peppers by the spoonful; the curved back of a Hegel chair; the sudden height and disappearing steel of the St. Louis Arch; a hot bursting blueberry after it's baked; the burn at the back of my throat from caramel bourbon; the drift of Himalayan sea salt to sop up light green oil on bread. I want the 70s back, all of it. I want velvet crush socks and cashmere panties; black truffle dust; the low dusky sound of the bass. I want the soft full hand of my mother resting in my hand. I want. I want. I want.

Blue Physics

The locals pointed me between the trees
toward the beach.
It wasn't much of anything,
a thin strand, fumble of rocks and seaweed.

How or why, I walked so far? To escape
our workshop group,
the poem about a lover's death.

I returned with a cup,
blue plastic whale jumping
out of its open mouth.
Natural Blue was playing in
the bar where I saw him drowning.

Why is blue so rare in nature?
If you zoom in on a Morpho-wing butterfly
light bends through air into another material
making the wings appear blue.

The sky when I saw you,
like the fish in the blue tank,
in a bar filled with laughter,
filled with air you couldn't breathe.
I tried to turn every head, get you out,
both of us wide-eyed and screaming.

I've Been Trying to Pay Attention

The way I did when I'd ride in the back
        of my father's car while he drove through

Brooklyn, light flipping through the slats
        in the train track overpass. The tremor from

metal wheels entering me
        through the open windows.

I'd squint my eyes and what passed before
        me was color-woven, undulating like a flag,

light kissing my lids—my mother singing
        in her soft soprano. Where are you now?

Light, light, light. I close my eyes and there,
        I'm in the back seat again. My father's hands curved

around the wheel and my mother gesturing
        toward the sky. You see, it's just a small blue nest.

Look here at the brunt edges of the tulip leaves fat
        and full of rain, and here at the split walnut trees

in your yard that when backlit look like broken hearts.
        Open your mouth wide when you bite the sun,

you'll want to feel it yolk,
        then radiate—radiate—radiate.

My Husband Holds Up a Pair
of Mismatched Socks

I tell him not to worry, eventually they will
find their match.

Eventually this wind will give way to silence
and what's more

the fox is back and she is alone.
The rooster has survived the winter—

Just listen to that crowing.
Your keys? Haven't touched them,

but if you look in the top drawer,
of your father's old bar they might be there.

This morning is about surrender,
a morning that lets the weeds take over.

Just look at those white clouds the size of Bowhead whales,
supplying at least half the oxygen you breathe.

Continue to seek what is lost,
or buried, or sit with me

and enjoy the dew lacing itself
over the lawn, allowing the Dandelions

to burst into flower, feeding the bees,
which is when I hope, you will forgive me,

for storing the hard-boiled eggs,
in the blue bowl, with the raw.

Lesson

A bee between 2 sunlit panes,
        squirrels hyper in the dry leaves.

As we cleave to one another,
        I know we have accepted death,

too tired to outrun it,
        so we tug at the nasty rattle

that we know will one-day sink
        its sharp teeth into our skin

and as that bite swells and the venom
        spreads neither one of us will be able to

move or speak. Who will need words then?

April is the Cruelest

Reminder of what
      will not sprout

out of frozen
      ground, burst

from twisted
      branches

call from
      the distant kitchen

to curse
      the empty milk carton.

Notes:

"Falling" owes tribute to Anne Lamott's essay, *"School Lunches"* remembering that boy by the fence.

"Spotting," song lyrics from Janet Jackson's Pleasure Principle.

"Freaks like Us" quotes Alfred Lord Tennyson's "Nothing Will Die." The poem is dedicated to the artist, Allison Delisi.

"Gettysburg," owes tribute The Decemberist's, *This is Why We Fight*. The last line owing tribute to Anne Carson's poem, *XXIV. AND KNEELING AT THE EDGE OF THE TRANSPARENT SEA I SHALL SHAPE FOR MYSELF A NEW HEART FROM SALT AND MUD.*

"Tangerine" title owes tribute to Led Zeppelin, as well as the line, *"Measuring a summer day,"* lyric from the song of the same name.

"Abecedarian," mentions, "Only The Good Die Young" by Billy Joel.

"Body Parts Messenger" is for Vincent Buschi Jr.

"Memento Mori" translation from Latin, 'Remember you must die.'

"Train Ride Through Small Towns" is an Ekphrastic poem based on Edward Hopper's "Compartment C Car," 1938.

"I Want" owes tribute to William Blake's print, "I Want, I Want" which was an expression of his desire for space.

Erasure from an article in Buffalo News, July 1, 1991

The poem "Cactus" is for Leslie Blanchard.

"The Day we Heard," Last line owes tribute to Laura Kasischke

"Blue Physics" owes tribute to Julie Bryne's song, Natural Blue.

"April is the Cruelest" owes tribute to T.S. Eliot's, "The Wasteland."

Translations from Italian:
Sogni Doro, from "Last Will and Testament" means sweet dreams.

"My Mother Too Grief Stricken to Mother": *Silenzio non piangere*,
Silence don't cry. *Guarda in alto, c'è un dio che ti ama*, Look up there's
a god who loves you. *Non sei solo*, You are not alone.

"Gettysburg" was included in a chapbook, Tightwire (2016).

Acknowledgements:

2River: "Grey History," "Terrified for this World"
Anti-Heroin Chic: "The Day Room"
The Banyan Review: "The Day we Heard"
Chestnut Review: "I Want"
Cloudbank: "Last Will & Testament"
Dodging the Rain: "Lesson Plan"
Dream Pop: "In Case of Emergency"
Figure 1: "Body Parts Messenger"
Glacier: "Baby Shower"
Gyroscope Review: "The Ice Storm"
Indolent Books: "Snake a Drain," "Freaks Like Us" (Earlier Versions)
The Laurel Review: "The Day we Didn't (Tension)", "Memento Mori I. II."
Lily Poetry Review: "Spring"
Liminal Spaces: "Union of Heaven and Earth"
MER: Spotting, "I Saw a Girl"
Midway Journal: "Cactus"
The Night Heron Barks: "Tangerine"
On the Seawall: "Abecedarian"
One Art: "Turning"
Ploughshares: "Falling"
River River: "Gettysburg"
Rough Cut: "Blue Physics"
Sheila-Na-Gig: "The Cyclone," "Coda: Independence Day" (Earlier version)
Stirring: "The Head"
Sweet Lit: "My Husband Holds Up a Pair of Mismatched Socks"
Thimble: "Train Rides Through Small Towns"
West Trestle: "Kiss Kill"

Gratitude

Thank you to Michelle Butler who always drops everything to find inspiration in my poems in order to make art. My deepest gratitude to my first readers, Jeff Butler and Rebecca Barry, and to the editors who gave earlier versions of these poems a home. I also want to thank Joan Kwon Glass for reading and editing a much earlier version of this book and to my students who inspire me to keep it real everyday. Finally, this book would not exist and would not be shaped or even seen by me without the care, guidance, and keen eye of Eileen Cleary. Eileen, you continue to be a force. To Martha Mccollough whose patience is unmatched. Thank you for carefully building this collection and for designing the cover.

About the Author

Mary Lou Buschi's collections of poetry are *Paddock* (Lily Poetry Review Books 2021), *Awful Baby,* (Red Paint Hill 2015), and 3 chapbooks: *Ukiyo-e, Tight Wire,* and *The Spell of Coming (or Going).* Mary Lou holds an M.F.A. in poetry from the M.F.A. Program for Writers at Warren Wilson College and a Master of Science in Urban Education from Mercy College. Her poems have appeared in many literary journals such as *Ploughshares, Glacier, FIELD, Willow Springs, Indiana Review, Radar, Tar River, Cream City, Rhino, The Laurel Review,* among others. She lives in Nyack, NY and is a full-time special education teacher in the Bronx. Her preferred pronouns are she/her.

www.ingramcontent.com/pod-product-compliance
Lightning Source LLC
Chambersburg PA
CBHW031251120626
46545CB00007B/2766